Rhyme and Reason
Poetry Inspired by Science

Kate Rauner

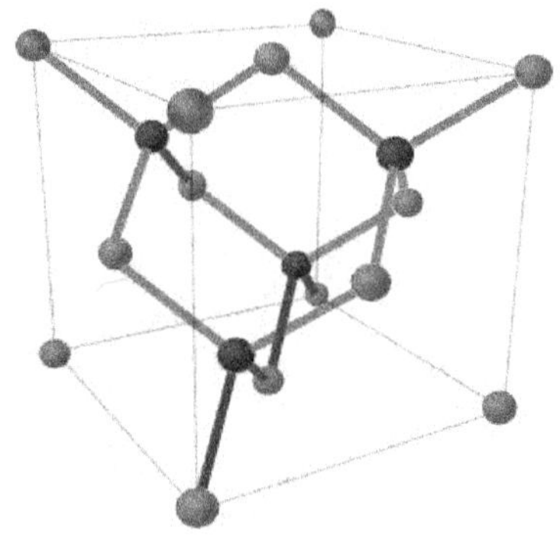

ii

Poet's Note

"Poets say science takes away from the beauty of the stars – mere globs of gas atoms. I too can see the stars on a desert night, and feel them. But do I see less or more? The vastness of the heavens stretches my imagination – stuck on this carousel my little eye can catch one-million-year-old light. A vast pattern - of which I am a part… What is the pattern, or the meaning, or the why? It does not do harm to the mystery to know a little about it. For far more marvelous is the truth than any artists of the past imagined it. Why do the poets of the present not speak of it? What men are poets who can speak of Jupiter if he were a man, but if he is an immense spinning sphere of methane and ammonia must be silent?" *Richard Feynman*

Richard Feynman was one of the most important physicists of the 20th Century; certainly, he was the most interesting. I take his words as a challenge to poets everywhere. This book collects some of the poems I wrote to meet his challenge and write poems inspired by science.

I favor rhyme and short phrases in my poems. These match a poem to the rhythm of my steps, which is inevitable since I frequently compose while walking. I also enjoy the discipline that rhyme imposes. It pleases my analytical mind when the perfect word presents itself, fitting both the poem's subject and its form.

My poems are meant to be fun. You will find no existential angst here. Writing poetry makes me happy, and I hope you'll share a bit of my happiness as you read.

These poems have all appeared previously on my blog. Search Kate Rauner Wordpress

It's an unusual name, you'll find me

Many of these poems were revised for this book. You may read my latest efforts there along with posts about my science fiction books and thoughts on science news. I look forward to your visits and your comments.

-- *Kate*

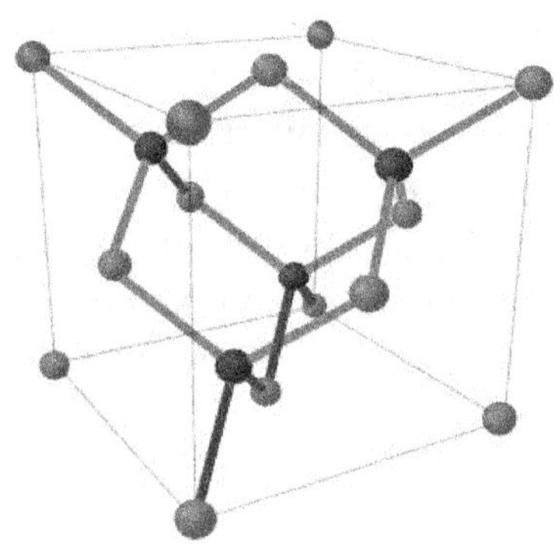

Table of Contents

Physics

"It does not do harm to the mystery to know a little
about it. For far more marvelous is the truth than any
artists of the past imagined it." *Richard Feynman*

~ ~ ~

Atomic Tea

Your cup of tea sits quietly,
Its surface still and calm.
A tiny wisp of steam
Is all that's going on.
Now magnify your vision,
Expand the scale up.
A cup as big as planet Earth
With atoms big as cups.
Tea is a glob of atoms,
Each jiggling in the heap.
Atoms that are water
And jiggling that is heat.
Cup-atoms block tea-atoms,
Despite how fast they seem.
But if tea-atoms hit the air
They pop right out as steam.
Hot tea-atoms jiggle fast -
Move randomly in air.
If they jiggle back to tea,
They're stuck again in there.
Now blow away the steam -

Atoms can't return to tea.
Hot atoms still keep popping out;
Removing heat, you see.
And so atomic theory
Allows your mind to see:
If tea's too hot for you to sip
Then blow to cool your tea.

*In honor of Richard Feynman, I begin this collection
with six poems inspired by his book Six Easy Pieces.
This first poem is inspired by Lecture 1: Atoms in
Motion.*

~ ~ ~

Fundamentals

The world we live in every day
We understand in many ways.
We simplify, amalgamate,
But mostly know things' speed and weight.
Know when the apple hits the ground,
Know red hot steel and waves of sound.
But all these rules are incomplete.
They can't describe the quantum leap.
Here's where Newton's world goes bust,
Electric light is waves and pulse,
Space-time's the force of gravity,
And particles move uncertainly.
Experiment tells us something's so –
If testing shows – then it *is* so!
We may not want a world like that -
It's horrible,
But that is that.

*From Richard Feynman's book Six Easy Pieces,
Lecture 2: Basic Physics*

Sciences

Chemistry,
Biology,
We study these.
Astronomy,
Geology,
For tools we need.
Hydrometeorology,
For lives we lead.
But physics –
Curiosity demands.

From Richard Feynman's book Six Easy Pieces,
Lecture 3: Relation of Physics to Other Sciences

~ ~ ~

It's a Fact

It is a fact in nature that energy's conserved.
The total's always constant, changing form, but not
perturbed.
Gravitational, potential, nuclear, kinetic,
Radiant and chemical, elastic and electric.
Existence gives mass energy, Einstein got us there.
Mass and energy relate: E=mc squared;
(That's when momentum is a null
From where you look to there.)
The energy so useful to power our machines
Is mathematical abstraction; reality as dreams.
Don't need to understand it all to pay electric bills,
And speak of it with confidence, and calculate at will.

From Richard Feynman's book Six Easy Pieces,
Lecture 4: Conservation of Energy.

Falling

Everything is always falling,
Falling everywhere.
It all seems so familiar
We don't see the mystery there.
What holds the Sun together,
What keeps his planets bound,
What pulls the tides through oceans,
Keeps my feet upon the ground.
It is the shape of space-time.
Through four dimensions fall.
So now we see the mystery,
Can it be a force at all?

*From Richard Feynman's book Six Easy Pieces,
Lecture 5: Theory of Gravitation
"Some major mysteries in physics have frustrated great
minds for decades, including the nature of ... gravity,
for which no particle has been found." Math 3*

How Can It Be So?

Run the tests over, with protocols tight,
Electrons alone, electrons and light.
You find it's uncertain, day after day,
If electrons are lumps, or electrons are waves.
They're both and they're neither, no one can explain.
This is what happens, the answer's the same.
It's thoroughly proven, nature's this way.
The math is so simple, the words fall away.
Don't try to fit
The results that you get
To your intuition,
No one's done it yet.
"Try not to ask,
'How can it be so?'
"No one knows
How it can be so."

From Richard Feynman's book Six Easy Pieces,
Lecture 6: Quantum Behavior.

Mars-ward Ho

Orbiting the planet,
  above Viking's bones,
Odyssey's a switchboard
  that seeks new landing zones.
Global Mars Surveyor
  measures gravity,
Magnetosphere, minerals,
  and topography.
MAVEN and Mangalyaan
  sniff at the Martian air,
Japan will gather samples
  and bring them back from there.
Joining Opportunity
  in studying the rocks,
Rover Curiosity
  seeks life's building blocks.
UAE will gather data
  on the frigid dry climate.
China's rover should be very good
  at biotech.
Sands of a planet solely occupied
  by robots,
Soon will carry boot-prints from
  eager astronauts.
Far beyond horizons
  where ancestors have roamed,
Mars One and SpaceX
  want to claim Mars as a home.

Haiku: Empty Space

Space between planets
Dark empty void that is full
Gluons and wonder

~ ~ ~

Brian's Spider

Waves across the universe
Ripple time and space,
While on the Earth a spider
Finds waves more to its taste.
Oh, to be so famous,
One of physics' best.
Oh, to be immortalized,
Known for your quantum quest.
Oh, to be so honored,
To have your name applied
To another bit of nature
That on a waveform glides.
A dark and leggy spider
That dives in southern ponds
Or strides across their surface
Until its prey is found.
Your name will ride, oh Brian Greene,
On waves of gravity,
Or maybe longer will endure
In a name that's spidery.

This poem is hard to categorize - like a lot of things in the universe. Physicist Brian Greene explains the discovery of gravity waves. He's a founder of World Science Festival, an annual event in New York City - alas, half a continent away from me - and for the first time in Brisbane, Australia - even farther.

Universe's Missing Piece

In all of creation,
In all the gains and losses,
There only are four
Universal
forces.
That's the Standard Model
Which for years has served so well
Predicting interactions
On the cosmic
carousel.
Yet something has been missing,
Something that evades,
Dark matter and dark energy
Beyond the model
strayed.
Oddly interacting
Are dark light's weak protons
That could be an anomaly
Or protophobic
bosons.
The ideas are exciting,
But confirmation's key
Before our minds can grasp
What makes up
reality.

A study in Physical Review Letters *indicates that a fifth fundamental force may exist.*

Astronomy and Space

"If you wish to make an apple pie from scratch, you must first invent the universe." *Carl Sagan*

~ ~ ~

We Are Made

Up, up, and down,
Quarks in a cloud
Are bound.
Quiescent, they coalesce; ignite;
Balance heat and mass;
Warm to yellow-white.
Proton, proton, proton chain,
Dense enough at zero age.
Ashes sink in orange flame.
Now expanding, heating more,
Bright red shell,
Collapsing core.
Until explosion, flares away
The nebula; all that remains
Is cooling dim and gray.
It will coalesce again
"We are made of
Starstuff,"
Says Carl Sagan.

With thanks to Hertzsprung and Russel, and Carl Sagan

North Star

The universe circles
And centers the sky
On the small bear's last star
To my northern eye.
But eons ago,
When writing was new,
The pyramid-builders
Looked at the sky too.
Their universe circled
Stars different from mine,
In the dragon's faint tail,
Fifth star in the line.
Far in the future
A worthier light
Will pivot the sky
For eyes in the night.
What manner of man?
Would woman we know?
When the universe circles
Round Vega's bright glow.

~ ~ ~

Solar Forge

A hundred Earths would fit across the sphere,
Except they'd boil away.
The energy of life blasts out, hurled
Into space, and will for eons untold.
Earth catches a drop in her blue hands and molds
Our world.
Geysers surge in jets and waves and looping flares,
Hotter than any gas.
Human hands blend metals forged in flame.

But only the Sun transmogrifies
In a forge with protons, neutrons,
Which lie beyond my eyes.
I only say their names.

~ ~ ~

Star Sugars

Via photosynthesis,
Plants store solar energy
In hydrated aldehydes,
Organics formed so cleverly.
Add nitrogen or phosphorus
For an acidic amide,
Defining protein molecules,
Solvents, enzymes, muscles, hide.
So why do interstellar clouds
Contain organic molecules?
Ubiquitous in dusty space
Where life can hardly be the rule?
There is compelling evidence,
Despite cold in extremity,
That cosmic rays are driving
An out-of-balance chemistry.
Unborn stars and planets
Laced with heavy elements
Are interstellar nurseries
For compounds biorelevant.

Planet Hunting

You can join the zooniverse;
For science you can do;
Space or climate, nature,
And exoplanets too.
When planets pass before a star,
Its light will dim and fall,
NASA posts the data:
Light curves are what they're called.
The human brain works wonderfully
For patterns to detect,
A treasure hunt for planets
That amateurs can get.
But if you want more data still
You can collect your own.
Find an exoplanet,
Be an amateur renowned.
From the NASA data,
Just select a likely star,
Then track its magnitude yourself
To seek a planet far.
You'll need to read and learn and then
You'll find you can begin.
You'll need a camera and a mount;
Filters, software, then
You'll need a telescope;
Find one you can afford;
And one more thing is needed,
In your planet-hunting hoard.
You'll want patience in abundance,
Because, night after night,
You'll record the magnitude,
Watch for that dip in light.
It helps to have some company,
And to be warmly dressed,

But what you need most, even more,
Is to be obsessed.

Interested? Visit planethunters.org or zooniverse.org

~ ~ ~

Creating Earth and Moon

Terrestrial and lunar rocks
Share similarities,
Some isotopes of elements
Are found in both of these.

Early in the solar system,
When proto-worlds collide,
Such isotopic matching
Is hard to reconcile.

New research seeks a better scheme
And everyone is trying,
Potassium in rocks may show
Which models are complying.

If the rogue colliding spheres
Vaporized Earth's mantle
To atmospheres of gaseous rock,
Of fluids supercritical,

Then Earth and Moon, upon their face,
Would match in just this way.
Their composition now makes sense
At least, it does today.

Broken Moons

The solar system was a dangerous place
Three billion years ago.
Protoplanets and icy debris
Hurtled to and fro.

Bent space with their masses,
Warped time as they flew,
Leaving behind
Crusts networked with clues.

It didn't require direct impact,
While those were common too,
Tidal encounters were all that it took
To rend a surface in two.

Life's a system so fragile!
We worry if temperatures rise.
We're shook by quakes and volcanoes,
But at least our crust won't divide.

I'm glad to be born in the relative calm
Since planets have cleared out their orbits.
Snuggled within a biosphere,
Not hammered by what came before it.

*Thanks to Alice Quillen (University of Rochester in
New York) et al for their new modeling study*

Center of the Universe

You've heard that space is expanding,
You've heard that science is sure
That galaxies fly from galaxies
For as long as time will endure.

But if space-time is expanding,
Just what's it expanding into?
What's beyond the edge of
The universe that we view?

Just more and more that we'll never see,
Each frame of reference is valid.
Each star at the center of everything
Regardless of how much is added.

So I might be forgiven for saying
That I stand in a special place,
That I am the center of everything,
Of energy, matter, and space.

*This poem gives me an excuse to believe I'm more
important that you are! Like Dr Suess's Yertle the
Turtle.*

How Mars Will Kill You

There could be solar flares
on the journey there,
Don't forget crash landings
could happen, to be fair.
Water's on the surface
but in a frozen brine.
Assume that you can purify
enough to drink in time.
The atmosphere is toxic
but there is more to heed.
It's less than one percent
of the pressure that you need.
Besides the lack of air,
no magnetic force surrounds,
So cosmic radiation
will force you underground.
Orange dust will be the bane
of your solar collectors,
Of moving parts and human lungs,
And of your airlock doors.
If your heating system fails
you will likely freeze,
And if you find your thumb's not green,
Starvation adds to these.
You better hope you like your fellows
and avoid some fights.
It would be a shame to kill
each other in the night.
Your life's a tough routine,
Your dangers aren't a thrill.
Mars is unrelenting.
With its slow-motion kill.

Exotic Space Weather, Far Away

Jupiter has its Great Red Spot
And now we find it's clear,
There's a bigger storm on a bigger world
A thousand light-years near.

Careening round its own star,
Locked to face one way,
It blows impressive winds
From endless night to always day.

Its clouds are flecked with minerals,
With rubies and sapphires.
If you think you'd die to see,
You would indeed expire.

Around the star HAT P dash seven,
In the constellation of the Swan,
Gems ride on sparkling winds
Round a planet with no dawn.

Eureka - Maybe

Earth first touched planet Mars
On the Golden Plain
When forty years ago
The search for life began.

Where barren outflow channels
From the Tharsis ridge
May once have carried water,
Where something might have lived.

Viking One took images,
Surveyed the dunes nearby
And analyzed geology
Beneath the pinkish sky.

Its tests for life seemed negative,
But we don't understand
Why something used the nutrients
Dripped on a bit of sand.

We've learned so much in forty years,
We know there are organics,
Maybe Viking did discover
A few cryptobiotics.

Starlight Speaks

Everything we know
About the universe
Comes from feeble twinkles
That speak grandly when observed.

When does the light arrive,
And comes from what direction?
How intense or diffuse
Are colors from refraction?

Light presents a barcode
Of dark lines to be read
Across the vibrant spectrum
From UV to infrared.

As starlight travels to the Earth
Each atom in the way
Leaves its mark within the beam
As photons fly away.

And so, we know how far's the star
How fast it moves past us,
If planets orbit 'round its disk
And what its core is made of.

Mars' Lost Chance

A shallow sea that shimmered
Beneath a sky of blue,
As promising a planet
As any that Earth knew.

A passing asteroid
Sheared off its northern pole,
Set Mars on a course
To barren, dry, and cold.

It ruined north-south symmetry,
The planet's never healed.
Destroyed cosmic protection
By its magnetic field.

Solar winds bombarded,
Air slowly was devoured
By protons and electrons
At a million miles an hour.

Mars clutched its air with gravity,
But that was not enough.
Its magnetosphere was shattered
And its molten core rebuffed.

A friendly little planet
That could have been a home
To our cosmic brethren
Has left us on our own.

Biology

"We are glorious accidents of an unpredictable
process." *Stephen Jay Gould*

~ ~ ~

Life on Europa

Endlessly squashed by Jupiter's mass,
Tides in rocks that flow like glass,
Heat of the core
bursts marine floors
And mineral teas
brew deep in the seas.
Sulfur and phosphates only in traces,
But rich with precursor acids and bases.
Organic foams
that slither and roam
While transparent tubes
trap colloidal foods.
Extremes of heat and pressure so benthic
What's possible must be chemosynthetic.
Free swimming ribbons
sport bio-glow fins,
Small shelly things
ooze membranes like wings.
Europa hosts life
deep under her ice -
Perhaps.

To Be Me

There are membranes in my cells
That limit-bound my organelles.
One carries DNA remote.
Yes, I am eukaryote.

I hold ancient seas inside
So in a brackish brew reside;
A chordate, backbone, and I breathe.
Yes, I am fish from ancient seas.

I swing my arms to move about,
With forward eyes in shortened snout.
I have flattened finger nails.
Yes, monkey with a remnant tail.

A harder question than these three:
What does it take? To be me?
A question I face every day
And hope to answer my own way.

~ ~ ~

Eohippus angustidens

Eohippus.
Dawn Horse.
What a perfect name
For the arch-backed little creature
That was horses' sire and dame.

But then a staid committee
That sets official names,
By earlier citation found

..... You to be

..... Hyracotherium

..... Hi - Ra - Ko - Ther - E- Um

I hated that decision;
Oh, I understand the rules.
Still *Eohippus* is so fine,
The name a splendid jewel.

But mixing clads made Hyra fail.
So beauty does prevail.

You're Eohippus pretty tooth
from nose to ropey tail.

Thanks to Stephen Jay Gould, an evolutionary biologist who studied land snails of the Caribbean and developed the theory of punctuated equilibrium with Niles Eldredge.

Horse According to Man

Since eighteen hundred seventy-nine
and Huxley's chart illustrious,
the story of evolving horse
has been passed down
to all of us.
                    Eohippus, Mesohippus, Protohippus, Equus.
                    Each with lesser toes and larger teeth
                                for grass ubiquitous.
Neat and tidy, moving up,
a story to betray,
from primitive to modern,
how progress is conveyed.

                            But Equus lingers only
                            as a remnant of the way,
                            its vibrant bush of species
                            has dwindled till today.

Merrychipus, Hypohippus,
three-toed feet sublime.
Pliohippus' single toe
did not erase their kind.

                            Four million years or more
                        they galloped happily through time:
                            Evolution as vivacious tree,
                                not ladder to be climbed.

There is another creature,
modern remnant of abundance,
lone surviving species
of diversity it showed once.
                            Now tries to draw life's journey
                                with a thumb in every fist,
                            and climbs a ladder reaching
                                    to only our hubris.

Inspired by Stephen Jay Gould's essay 'Life's Little Joke'.

Haiku: Bear

Hunter in the dark
You are seen by the hunted
A hungry day dawns

~ ~ ~

Platypusology

Victorians called her primitive,
A mammal under-done,
Chimera of cold austral streams,
Life's ladder, on a lower rung.

With lizard bones and otter fur
That's waterproof and soft as silk.
Laying eggs as lizards do,
Then nursing babes on milk.

She hunts her prey in bottom mud
With tactile snout exquisite;
More delicate than human touch,
She senses nerve cells with it.

Life branches out a thousand ways,
Ignores our human urge
For categories neat and trim;
Nature's on a splurge.

A creature that's most elegant,
Beauty's her attraction.
Admire now the platypus,
A honey of adaption.

Inspired by Stephen Jay Gould .

Dogs Go Woof, Cats Go Meow, Llamas Go...

Llamas hum when they're hungry,
They hum when they're bored,
They hum when they're nervous,
Or away from their herd.
They'll scream when they're fighting,
Or snort as they run,
But if you want to know
... how llamas go:
Llamas go hummm.

Inspired by my own herd.

~ ~ ~

Worried Dog

The dog is worried.
Cats come in.
They stalk his tail,
Squat by his bowl,
Leap on the table
Where he cannot go.
Foolish humans
See only plush fur,
Hear only soft purrs.
Not glowing eyes,
Prickly claws.
Don't hear
Creeping paws.
Foolish humans!
The dog is worried.

Based on my field observations of the very local fauna.

The Ape That Cooks

We are the hunting ape,
But other apes do hunt.
We are the speaking ape,
But other apes do grunt.
What set us on the path
To our enormous brain?
And brought us down
From the trees
To walk across the plain?
We are the ape with fire!
There's evidence to show
Prometheus brought us his gift
A long *long* time ago.
With fire, sleeping on the ground,
Protected from the lions,
We shed our dense and furry coats,
It warmed us through the nighttime.
While other apes use their day
To chew and chew and chew
Their tubers, leaves, and wild fruits
We cooked the first
fast food.
This new step in digestion
Meant more calories,
Cooked out the germs and toxins
Of wild plants and meats.
Tied to our adaption,
We'd never be the same.
We are the ape that cooks,
The primates of the flame.

What do you think makes us human?

Cavern Bats

Rising from the cavern,
As swirling clouds,
As living smoke,
Spiraling up from the pit
Come the bats.

Tourists watch, still and silent.
Bats make no sound,
No chirp nor chatter,
No flap of wings
Comes with the bats.

No group can be silent for long.
Someone coughs,
Whispers,
A baby cries.
Still the bats come.

Feet shuffle
As a few people leave
Beneath the stream of wings.
A cricket trills its evening song.
Still the bats come.

Distant city lights glow,
On a plain beyond the cliffs.
People trickle away
Until less than half remain.
Still the bats come.

I no longer see them
Circling in the pit,
Only their silhouettes
Against the evening sky.
Still the bats come.

Stars begin to shine
High overhead.
The Summer Triangle,
The Northern Cross.
Still the bats come.

Darker now.
Too dark for my eyes
To see a bat against the sky.
I rise.
I leave for that city's glow.
Still the bats come.

*Thanks to Carlsbad Cavern National Park and the USA
National Parks' Hundredth Anniversary*

Limusaurus, the Mud Lizard

As dinosaurs evolved to birds
Their teeth reduced and disappeared,
Though some kept jaw bones, jagged sharp -
A modern goose is to be feared!

Teeth seem to be so useful
To hunting and to dine
That penguins have a toothed tongue,
Some modern chicks grow oral spines.

One hundred million years ago
Limusaurs did not concur.
They dropped their teeth as adults grew,
A smooth beak they preferred.

Wholly unexpected
And never seen before,
Fossils show that babies would
Lose their teeth that tore.

More strange discoveries await
As fossils come to hand
To show us that surprising beasts
Once stalked across the land.

*When I watch a Road Runner hunting, I can easily
believe that birds are avian dinosaurs.*

America's Coyote

Coyote is our canid,
A true American,
For a million years
Remaining at his origin.

Coyote's always waiting,
Coyote's always hungry,
And so we have
Waged war on him
All across the country.

Kill half a million every year
On foot, in trucks, from planes,
But Coyote has found refuge
Where humans aren't his bane.

He spread from coast to coast,
From plains to cities, towns,
To parks, and urban sprawl,
He builds himself a home.

He thrives on rats and mice
That follow mankind's rise,
Absorbing genes from wolf and dog,
That's how Coyote thrives.

America's own avatar,
Our native totem beast.
Howl out your anthem,
May your singing never cease.

I've been intrigued by stories of coyotes' success
surviving rural attempts at extermination and now
moving into cities - the stories keep coming.

Crow's Funeral

The deceased lies before them,
The crowd cloaked all in black.
They're watching for the villain
Who may be coming back.

It's not known if they're mourning.
They do not shed a tear.
They watch and they remember,
In anger, what to fear.

Humans are unusual
In tending to their dead.

Elephants, chimpanzees,
And porpoises, it's said,
Will touch and groom,
Seem agonized,
But do they soon forget?

Only corvids, of the birds,
Gather for a wake
And surround a murdered friend.
What vengeance will they take?

*Studies show that crows recognize human faces and
will follow a person who raided their nests, screaming
and even diving at the villain.*

Mysterious Jungle Mounds

Deep in Columbian jungles
Rise mysterious mounds,
Twice as high as humans stand,
No one knew what they had found.

Seen from the air,
they're puzzling.
Are they what Mayans leave?
Or built by ancient farmers?
By Spanish? or ETs?

Reality is better
Than any fantasy,
And crazy,
As I understand
The real world,
'Cause, gee,
Nature sure is grand!

Now we've finally got the scoop!
It's earthworm poop,
It's earthworm poop.
In the deepest jungles rise
Piles and piles of earthworm poop.

Gee, nature is grand!

"It's a fantastic paper—really exciting and compelling findings," published May 11, 2016 in the journal PLOS ONE.

Flowers Saved Forever

I have petals from my love
Pressed tween the pages of a book,
And rose buds given to me once
Dried in a jar, so not forsook.

They'll last a decade, maybe more,
Perhaps a lifetime treasured,
Then be consigned into the trash,
My sentiment be measured.

Ephemeral my life may be,
Its meaning soon will disappear,
But some mementos of the past
Outlast me by a million years.

Millennia evolving
Since flowers first appeared,
Are preserved for human eyes,
Eternity in amber tears.

I will send my precious bud
Beyond the reach of my dead hand,
Encased within a blob of resin,
Buried deep in thickening sand.

Solstice Star in the Grass

A solstice moon has washed away
Starlight from up high,
Leaving Mars and Jupiter
To dominate the sky.

But there's a tiny blue-white star,
A fleck of light below,
Nestled in the parched-dry grass
That gives a steady glow.

Rare the sight in my backyard,
This pale beetle's essence,
As wonderful as any star
Is bioluminescence.

Pressures vast drive fusion
And spark atomic fires,
While at my feet, luciferin
Lights a bug's desire.

A star will shine a billion years,
This bug a night or two.
Yet it will breed another life
As sure as stars will do.

Every year I see a scant few glow beetles at my New
Mexico mountain home - only for a few nights around
the solstice, just before the monsoon rains begin

An Immortal Creature Sits Upon Your Thumb

Do you want to live forever?
Have immortality?
Existing in a cyborg mind
At the singularity?
Humans often end up cursed
When begging gifts from gods.
Beware of this approach,
You'll find it to be flawed.
From deadly cinnabar,
Don't brew a magic vector.
No seek the golden apples,
Or Milk Ocean's sweet nectar.

A simple little polyp
Achieves your heart's desire.
Will not decline with age,
It's life force does not tire.

Could sit upon your thumbnail,
This tiny glove of tentacles,
Forever totipotent,
It's mostly made of stem cells.

As long as it's not eaten,
In clean pond water's flow,
The hydra mocks your fondest dream
And doesn't even know.

*I love to watch scientists follow their data, even when it
leads away from their hypotheses: "I started my original
experiment wanting to prove that hydra could not have
escaped aging," said Daniel Martinez, a Pomona College
biologist. "My own data has proven me wrong — twice... I
do believe that an individual hydra can live forever under
the right circumstances."*

Haiku: We Mocks yur Gravity

All kittens can fly
Gravity waits patiently
Till they're old and fat

If I Could Have a Second Life

Ravens flying high
Calling, diving, barrel-roll
Have more fun than I

~ ~ ~

Natural GMO

What never lives
But yet evolves?

Retaines itself
In species broad?

Shares DNA
But never sex?

Familiar beast
You don't expect?

*Researchers from Boston College, US, are studying an
ancient group of retroviruses that affected many
modern mammal ancestors 30 million years ago.*

*Viruses colonized our ancestors and, "Over the course
of millions of years, however, viral genetic sequences
accumulate in the DNA genomes of living organisms,
including humans."*

Environment

"It's not what you look at that matters, it's what you
see." *Henry David Thoreau*

~ ~ ~

My Boots Carry Me

Push my foot snug in the shell of the toe,
Shove heel in with a 'schloop' as it goes.
Laces clip-clipping thru D-rings of brass
Are hooked through an open-backed rivet at last.
Taut but not tight, crisscrossed on the tongue,
Lodging each foot once travel's begun.
Walking through embers or wading thru floods,
Across boulder fields or curls of dried mud,
Meadows of flowers and valleys of grass,
A wind-blasted saddle, a steep mountain pass.
Pounding a cadence, my feet keeping time
Through miles of thoughts and hours of rhyme.
The beat of my heart is the rhythm of words.
Hiking's a metronome
Felt but not heard.

I Love Storm Clouds

Powered by sunlight that traveled through space,
Tumbling up from a wet heavy base,
Warm air and cold air parcels collide,
Dynamics and moisture heaped in the skies,
Piled by mountains above the terrain,
Clawing the ground with fingers of rain,
Strong sudden downdrafts spreading below
Bending the trees in cooling outflow,
Pouring down energy, all through the night,
Measuring distance with thunder and light.
I love storm clouds.

~ ~ ~

Haiku: Leaves #1

Autumn cool and damp
Fallen leaves sweet underfoot
Lead into winter

Leaves #2

Leaves all veiled in green
Drop their disguise in autumn
Unmask red and gold

"Carotenoids are present in leaves the whole year round, but their orange-yellow colors are usually masked by green chlorophyll. As autumn approaches, certain influences inside and outside the plant cause the chlorophylls to be replaced at a slower rate than they are being used up. During this period, with the total supply of chlorophylls gradually dwindling, the "masking" effect slowly fades away." Wikipedia

Spring Melt

 Spring time melts the snow
Icy threads weave through dark pine
Braiding white with black

~ ~ ~

River's Ghost

A civil river runs today,
Flows wide and calm near quaint cafes,
Flows gently past well-tended homes
Along the yards all freshly mown.

Tourists sprawl upon its back
To float in tubes and tow six-packs.
But early in the dawn there's still
The spirit of its ancient thrill.

Fog races water to the sea
And shows its wild side to me.
Flowing faster than the stream,
Turbulent as it careens
Against the shore in silent waves
To undercut the bank it made.

Up road footings, curling high,
Silent crashing on the sides.
Watch the fog and you will see
A river's ghost that once was free.

Inspired by the Delaware River at Port Jervis, New York.

Wildfire

The fire roared, it flew, it crowned
In this neighborhood at the edge of town.
It leaped and danced down streets of homes
To drive us to our safety zones.
Now flashing lights obscured by smoke
Mark engine crews still hard at work.
My hand crew seeks out embers red,
And digs them out to stop their spread.
With families gone and power off
The night is dark for houses lost.
It's oddly peaceful, hushed and calm.
Sadly that will not last long.
Tonight, the crews in green and gold
Walk through the tales that won't be told.
We do our job, but hear our warning
Of tears that will come in the morning.

*I'm a volunteer firefighter, now retired. Houses don't
have to burn. Learn about defensible space.
http://www.firewise.org/ It's not fate, it's your
responsibility.*

~ ~ ~

Haiku: Beauty in the Bone

Essence of the form
Buried under flesh and fur
Beauty of the bones

*Here in the forests of New Mexico's mountains, we all
come across interesting bones. Everyone has a few on
their porch.*

Elephants Phone Ahead

Tamil Nadu, India,
Where wildlife still roams,
Protected Asian elephants
Have trampled village homes.

A couple people every year
Have died in these locations,
But none at all were killed last year
Crossing tea plantations.

They can sign up
For text alerts
Or hear a spoken message,
See lights on towers flashing high
When elephants make passage.

Rangers then escort the folks,
Or they may walk away.
Teams of plantation workers, too,
Prevent a deadly day.

Instead of calls to slay the herds,
People now say, leave them.
We'll cross the tea plantation groves
Safely in the ev'nings

Elephants move from one patch to another at dusk
when workers are walking home from tea plantations.
In the growing darkness, even an elephant is hard to
spot, and a startled elephant will charge.

Haiku: Grasses #1

Seeds like banners raised
Tickling my fingertips
On an autumn stroll

Grasses #2
Clouds of purple seeds
Each drop drizzles through my hands
Soon to sleep in snow

~ ~ ~

More Life's Coming

Life's arising on Earth
Took conditions fairly rare,
Yet as the universe matures
Life could be everywhere.

With star formation winding down,
Supernovae will dwindle,
Small dim stars multiply,
More room for life to wiggle.

Impatient were our ancestors
Or maybe we're just lucky
Self-replicating molecules
Simply weren't too fussy.

Earth may be a pioneer
With most life in future-tense,
Good news for astrobiologists
Five billion years hence.

Haiku: Sun Pillar

Coming winter storm
Sends a pillar to heaven
In the early dawn

Learning

"It doesn't matter how beautiful your theory is, it doesn't matter how smart you are. If it doesn't agree with experiment, it's wrong." *Richard Feynman*

~ ~ ~

Reality's a Mess

A sphere is the most perfect shape
But Earth's an oblate pear.
Beautiful orbits are circular
But ellipses are what's there.
A species should be distinct,
Breed true, you must concur,
But lines evolve as time moves on,
Distinctions start to blur.
The speed of light is constant,
As every student knows,
But that's only in a vacuum
Or we wouldn't have rainbows.
Nuclear forces strong and weak
With particles unite,
By when will gravity join in
To end the physics fight?
Perfection is what's beautiful,
But reality stands the test.
Reality will always win,
And reality's a mess.

Thanks to Isaac Asimov's inspiration for kicking off this poem.

Today's a Good Day

Today's a good day
'Cause I learned something new,
A piece of the world I love
That I never knew.
       Learning something that
       I never will regret,
       Though what's discovered can be tough,
       Upsetting to accept.
With pain and delight,
Knowledge conveys
Twists and turns
Found in a maze…
       Of what I learn
       Some facts for myself.
       Some simply for fun
       Dolls on a shelf.
First comes science
For knowing the world,
From tightening screws
To a cosmos unfurled.
       Beauty's important,
       And so there is art
       To comfort my soul
       Or just for a lark.
I study ethics:
I want to be good,
To belong to mankind
And my own neighborhood.
       There's no guarantee
       On the learning I get.
       It's wrong on occasion
       Not complete or correct.
I will keep questing
To find what is true.
Today's a good day
'Cause I learned something new.

Wrong and Wronger

Answers can be right or wrong,
Or so we're taught in school.
Close answers that get closer still,
In science, that's the rule.

The teacher says "spell sugar".
I say s-h
u-g-r.
But if you spell it p-j-q,
I'm righter than you are.

Newton's laws were not disproved
When Einstein came along.
They still apply within their frame,
So Newton was not wrong.

Right keeps getting righter
As science goes on longer.
If you think that doesn't count,
You're wrongest of the wronger.

With thanks to Isaac Asimov again.

Age of Humanity

Our numbers and our industry,
Fossil-fuels and farming,
New minerals called pottery -
Are bricks and glass alarming?

Chemicals that we create,
Plastics, fibers, microbeads -
Mining moves three times more silt
Than all Earth's rivers can succeed.

Greenhouse gases, mass extinction,
And synthetic fertilizer,
Pesticides and GMOs,
Prove natural rate of change a miser.

Only since the last Ice Age
Came a Totally
New Epoch.
We have grown civilized
And now see where that has led us.

Epochs used to last for ages,
Now the Holocene,
Only twelve millennia old,
Yields to - Anthropocene.

We humans mark the planet,
We humans modify,
We humans are the greatest cause,
We're fruitful and we multiply.

When Living in the Physical World

If you're only skeptical,
If you always doubt,
Ideas never make it through.
Where's the joy of something new?
But if you are gullible
You'll fill your head with trash.
If ideas all are equal
Your thoughts are so much treacle.
You needn't choose between
A cynic or a dupe.
When living in the real world
Avoid approaches too absurd.
There is a way that does it
In a balance most exquisite -
Scrutinize hypotheses,
Stay open to the novelties.

I was reminded of Carl Sagan's fine advice at
Brainpickings.

~ ~ ~

Haiku: Cliff Dwelling

Ancient eyes once watched
Hands long gone build up stone walls
Where children did laugh.

Daily Mathematics

My grocery store is only
A twenty-minute drive,
A statement based on distance,
Relating speed and time.
You understand my drive at once,
It causes you no fuss.
Who says you don't comprehend
Integral calculus.

~ ~ ~

Geometry at Night

A holy city worshipped bulls
Two thousand years ago
And gave the world astrology,
Or so the story goes.
Masters of geometry
They watched the sky at night,
Saw lights that moved in retrograde
And puzzled at the sight.
Movements of the planets
Produce a twisted dance,
They charted it with dents in clay
And had no proper graphs.
Geometry was once supreme
Before the calculus.
Trapezoids drawn in the sky
For brains that functioned thus.

*Geometry is different. Some people connect with
geometry even if other forms of math leave them cold.
Cuniform tablets predicted planet motions with fancy
geometry found nowhere else in the ancient world.*

O Pluto, Pluto! Wherefore art thou

Tis but a moniker that yields strife;
Thou art thyself, though not a planet.

What's planet? It is nor rock,
nor atmosphere,
Nor dwarf, nor comet,
Nor bow wave in the solar winds.

But intermediate twixt them all,
and unique,
Orbiting the Sun.
Retain that dear perfection
And doff attempts to classify.

Oh, be some other thing!
That which we call a rose
By any other name
Would smell as sweet.

With apologies to The Bard

Witness Most Intimate

It saw the Colonies
Become United States,
Saw hostilities
Building as a cloud.
Heard the Independence
Declaration read out loud.

Captured Chinese porcelain,
Some German tankards, too,
Fragments of a window pane,
And bottles that held brew.

Heard revolution planned
By drunken
Patriots,
Wondered if the wine and beer
Birthed the outcome
That they got.

Held punch bowls and glasses,
Smoking pipes and dishes,
And bottles, bottles, bottles
For every drinker's wishes.

Served men and fallen ladies,
It was the privy pit
Of an illegal pub,
A Revolution's toilet.

*From archeologists digging on the future site of
Philadelphia's Museum of the American Revolution.*

Fifty Million Years Ago
East Asian Sea Plate at the Philippine Sea

Earth's history runs deep,
Hundreds of miles
Where seismic waves flow through the rock
As light waves through the air.

Ancient surface plates
That sunk beneath the crust
Last saw the sun when dinosaurs
Died in ash and dust.

Subducted shallow seas
Converged and disappeared.
Captured earthquake waves
Now show their forms
After fifty million years.

Surveillance

Eyes in the sky,
Eyes on the ground,
Eyes watch empty streets
And where crowds are found.

What makes you safer?
What feels right?
Open on internet,
Or restricted tight?

Watched through the night,
Watched dawn and noon.
You do need protection
But protection from whom?

Answer the Call

A call in the nighttime
Blasts me from my dreams,
Someone's in trouble
The radio does scream.

Don gear at the station
Climb into a truck,
To find the right driveway
Can sometimes be pure luck.

I've done this before,
I trust I'll be okay,
Now I'm running *towards*
While others run *away*.

My fate is in my hands
Thanks to training that I choose,
My equipment and my team
Mean *win* rather than *lose*.

Sure, it takes my time,
Puts me in some danger,
But I keep volunteering,
Help neighbor and help stranger.

*I'm retired now, but served as a volunteer firefighter for
many years.*

Final Thought

"We are at the very beginning of time for the human race. It is not unreasonable that we grapple with problems. But there are tens of thousands of years in the future. Our responsibility is to do what we can, learn what we can, improve the solutions, and pass them on." *Richard Feynman*

About the Poet

Kate Rauner is a retired Cold War Warrior. She worked for over twenty years at the Rocky Flats Plant, part of the nation's nuclear weapons complex. After the Cold War fizzled out, she switched to environmental engineering and project planning during the lengthy clean-up of the plant, which is now a wildlife refuge. "I've held plutonium in my hands," she says. "Not many people can say that."

Kate next moved to southwest New Mexico and worked at the copper mines around Silver City, a mining district since Native Americans collected copper there before the Spaniards entered Mexico.

Today she lives outside Silver City at the edge of the Gila National Forest with her husband and cat. She enjoys hiking and bird-watching, and, when serving as a volunteer firefighter, fought wildland and home fires. She writes science fiction and poetry. "I'm well on my way to achieving my life's goal," Kate says. "To become an eccentric, old woman."

Links in This Book

A few url links are included in this book, which were all working when the manuscript left my hands. Alas, the Internet is a fickle beast and some will be broken by the time you read this. Try searching on the poem's keywords and you should learn more.

-- *Kate*

Connect With Kate

See my books and find a Contact Me tab at
KateRaunerAuthor.Wordpress.com